DAD!

Don't throw your gum out the window!

DAD | DAUGHTER
MIKE SCHWEPPE, M.Ed. | EMILY SCHWEPPE-RUSHING, M.Ed.

ISBN: 979-8-9867613-0-5

Library of Congress Control Number: 2022944381

Contents

Preface

In 2011, when the content of our father-daughter conversations began to deepen, we found ourselves - for the first time - broaching topics like self-awareness, suffering and joy. After sharing some of our conversations and insights with others, we learned they'd been incorporating what we shared into their own lives.

In response to this feedback, six years later in 2017, we began yet another conversation: the choice to write a book; a decision that ultimately led us to reflect on the evolution of our relationship as dad and daughter -- from a hierarchy with a father thinking he knew best to a relationship based on mutuality, where Love honors the essence of each other's souls.

This book is a collection of nine of our most impactful father-daughter conversations, coupled with our own unique and individual perspectives on those talks. Our intention is to simply share our experiences and perhaps provide you with a starting point to begin deepening and transforming your own relationships via new conversations. We invite you to listen to our stories with an open heart, to reflect upon what most resonates with your own inner truth, and most importantly: to question everything we say because as the wise spiritual teacher Tony De Mello has taught us, only you know what's best for you.

Mike & Emily,

Cincinnati, OH

July 2022

Acknowledgements

We have so much gratitude for our family. In particular, thank you Sue/mom, for your open heart, your vulnerability, your courage, and your blessing for us to share our journey. Thank you for your inspiration, for your unconditional love and support, and for your powerful insights.

Thank you, Sarah. Two and a half years in, we were unsure of how to best convey what we wanted to say. Your third-force energy of reconciliation shifted everything for us. Your powerful questions created a dynamism we are so grateful for. Without you, Sarah, this book would not be what it is.

Thank you, Christy for reminding us that this is just our experience and everyone has their own path. And thank you for always making us laugh.

Thank you, Matt, for Taking a Stand.

Thank you, Sharon Finch, for your friendship, guidance and love.

With all our love and gratitude,

Mike & Em

x

Dedication

This book is dedicated to the late Tony deMello (9-4-31 to 6-2-87), whose words have been a common thread through our conversations for the past ten years. His recorded "Wake Up to Life" conference at Fordham University in 1987 has been a core teaching for us in becoming more self-aware. Thank you Tony for many things, but especially for helping us to finally see that when we change, everything and everyone changes.

Foreword

When I received an invitation from my sister and my dad to assist them with writing a book about their relationship, at first I was hesitant. Work on a book *about* my family *with* my family and try to remain objective so that I could be their writing coach? *Was this possible? Or even ethical? Was I insane?*

Despite my mind's attempts to dissuade me from even considering the project, I agreed to a meeting to discuss my potential involvement.

On the day of the meeting, I remember feeling a bit nervous. I imagined the minefield of triggers this project might have hidden for me. I wondered *how* would I feel? *What* would I feel? What feelings would they feel? What if I disagreed with them? And at the end of the day: was I willing to openly revisit the emotional content of my family's history and feel whatever feelings came up as a result?

When I entered the meeting with my sister and my dad that day, I noticed chapters from their book printed and taped to the walls. As I walked through the room, reading various excerpts and stories from my family's history, tears filled my eyes. These tears, however, weren't so much an expression of sadness or happiness, but instead the kind that seemed to be saying: *yes, right here, this is exactly where you're meant to be.*

As I continued reading through the chapters, I felt a sense of curiosity about not only what Emily and my dad had created, but the relationship they had with each other. I was drawn to their energy, their connection, and the impact I imagined their book could have on others who also wanted to deepen their relationships with family. Despite my fear, my desire to create something new with my dad and my sister was bigger: I wanted in.

We met twice each week over the next year and a half. Our writing process was simple, but not always easy. Ultimately, I was right: revisiting my family's history with my family did tend to elicit big feelings. It turns out, however, the very thing I was the most afraid of - feeling my feelings and truthfully sharing them with my family - was the thing I wanted the most.

If you're feeling curious about what might be possible in your relationships, a nudge to connect in a new way, or simply a desire to break free of the habitual unconscious patterns of relating in your family, I hope that you find reading this book to be as supportive and transformational as I experienced through the process of helping to create it.

Sarah Schweppe, MSSA, LISW, CHWC

The Formula

"There is only one cause of unhappiness: the false beliefs that you have in your head, beliefs so widespread, so commonly held, that it never occurs to you to question them."

- Tony deMello

A Methodology for Happiness

Every night after nine-year-old Emily brushed her teeth and climbed into bed, she watched her ceiling fan spin while waiting to say her prayers with her parents. Her bedtime routine wasn't complete until they had held hands and prayed: "Dear God, thank you for the world so sweet, thank you for the food we eat, thank you for the birds that sing, thank you God for everything."

Because Emily's dad, Mike, was raised in a conservative Catholic family, passing on traditions such as prayer was important to him. He believed they instilled gratitude and faith. Mike also believed that in addition to prayer, this routine of one-on-one time was important for his kids.

As a kid, Emily loved praying and talking to God with her parents. What she wasn't all that fond of was going to church and Sunday school every single week.

"But Dad, I don't want to go," Emily whined one Sunday morning over the phone to her dad. She was at her friend's house and didn't want to leave early. "Can't I just skip today pleeease?"

"We're on our way and you need to be ready," Mike replied.

Fifteen minutes later, Emily's family of six pulled up in their big white van. Emily knew getting out of church was a battle she was never going to win, so she got in the van, climbed over her three siblings into the back seat, and quietly held back her tears.

Regardless of how anyone felt about being there, it was Sunday and going to church was the expectation. After all, when Mike was a kid, he didn't get to decide whether or not he was going to church - so why would his kids?

DAD'S PERSPECTIVE ON THE FORMULA

As a young dad, I believed I had "the formula" for my kids' happiness, success, and path to heaven: play sports, go to church, graduate college, get a good job, get married, and have a family. When Sunday morning rolled around, there was no question that my kids would go to church, because in my mind, their success in life (and acceptance into heaven) depended on it. It was my responsibility to ensure these things happened.

Because my parents had the same formula for me, it never occurred to me that there could be a different way. As a result, for many years, I denied listening to any of my kids' opinions that challenged "the formula." After all, I am the dad, so "you will do as I say."

Tony deMello (referred to throughout this book as Tony or TDM) explains that these types of beliefs are the shadow of programming; the beliefs that are so ingrained into our being, that we never think to question them[1] (let alone allow our children to question them).

When I operate in the shadow of my programming and someone questions me, I react defensively. I get angry and resentful. As a young dad who was unaware of this programming, my reactive behavior often caused my children to run for the hills.

Tony goes on to say that we are born asleep, we are raised asleep, we get married asleep, we breed asleep and we die asleep.[2] Only when I became willing to look at how my unconscious programming negatively impacted me and my relationship with my family (twenty years after the Sunday morning church scrambles), did the grip of living my life "asleep" finally begin to loosen.

Today, as a result of questioning my own false beliefs, I see that, although formulas are necessary, they're never perfect. I believe that formulas have the ability to create guidance and structure, but when they are so rigid that we cannot see another way, we inhibit the flow of curiosity from our children. Ultimately we lose the opportunity to teach the importance of questioning.

Becoming aware of my programming has allowed me to question my habitual beliefs and behaviors. Most importantly, it has shifted my relationship with my children, because now there is space for everyone to speak their truth and ask questions - no matter how difficult they might be to hear.

Emily's Perspective on The Formula

As a kid, I always looked forward to hanging out with friends - playing games, riding bikes, and having slumber parties. If I was at a friend's house on Sunday morning, I'd often watch the clock as it crept closer to 11:00 a.m. - the time of our weekly church service and my Sunday school class. I secretly hoped my parents would forget that they had to pick me up for Sunday school.

Inevitably, however, I'd get the call from my parents: "Em, we're on our way to pick you up. You need to be ready."

As a kid, I had a hard time understanding this whole church thing. *Why couldn't I just skip it and hang out with my friends, I'd wonder. They didn't have to go to church. And besides, what really was the purpose of Sunday School anyway?*

Because I couldn't really question "the formula," I pretty much just went through the motions and did what my parents told me to do. There were things I enjoyed about church, like receiving communion and getting confirmed in eighth grade, but other than that, many of my prayers revolved around hoping my parents would forget about taking me on Sundays.

While my parents encouraged wonder and curiosity in many ways as a child, there was no room for questions regarding the unspoken "formula" for certain parts of how to live life. Come hell or high water, we were to be in the pews on Sunday, required to play sports, make every effort to get "good" grades in school, and then one day, get married and have kids. And repeat.

As a first grade teacher, I routinely notice children's natural born and unlimited curiosity. The never-ending "why" is something I welcome in my classroom: *Why do we need to learn this, Mrs. Schweppe? Why do we walk in a line? Why are the leaves green?*

Questions are ways for children to make sense of the world around them with the people they love and trust. They serve as opportunities to discover answers on their own. As TDM says, "it's infinitely more important to question than it is to simply swallow what is being said."

While I was not allowed to question "the formula," in many ways I am also grateful for it, because it instilled morals and values such as respect, faith, and gratitude. I believe it's equally necessary for children to have structure and guidance as it is to allow the freedom to question what they don't understand. Often this lack of ability to question leads kids to go through the motions in life without the curiosity and agency to find their own answers.

Without the freedom to question, we may unconsciously begin to rely on things outside of ourselves for our answers: a relationship, a career, the contents of a shopping bag, or a drink at the bar. And for as long as we stay stuck looking outside for our answers and our happiness, we will undoubtedly suffer.

Suffering

"Pain teaches a most counterintuitive thing: we must go down before we even know what up is. In terms of the ego, most religions teach in some way that all must 'die before they die.' Suffering of some sort seems to be the only thing strong enough to both destabilize and reveal our arrogance, our separateness, and our lack of compassion. I define suffering very simply as 'whenever you are not in control.'"

- Richard Rohr

Blanketed in Pain

Emily quietly cried in her bed one warm summer evening, listening to her parents yelling as her mom cried. The kitchen door slammed. Emily's mind raced, trying to make sense of the chaos: *Is one of them leaving? Will they come back? I don't want them to get divorced.*

At ten years old, Emily didn't understand the meaning of her parents' argument, but she did assume that she had caused it. *If only I could be good, maybe they wouldn't fight,* she thought. Clutching her security blanket, Emily tiptoed into her little brother's room; she knew being with the comfort of a sibling was better than listening to the shouts alone.

Lying on her brother's floor, Emily concluded that her dad must've been the one who made her mom cry; he must've been the reason she felt so sad. She felt anger toward her dad welling up inside of her. She tried to close her eyes to fall asleep, but the pain was too big for her little body to calm. She lay there, awake, with silent tears falling down her face.

Meanwhile, downstairs, Emily's parents had no idea their daughter was listening in and blaming herself for their intense emotions. When Mike and Sue fought over Sue's active drinking problem, all Mike could see was rage.

"WHY ARE YOU LYING TO ME? WHO ARE YOU? WHY CAN'T YOU JUST STOP DRINKING FOR OUR FAMILY?!" Mike screamed after finding another hidden bottle of vodka.

With quiet concern, Emily asked her mom if she was ok the next morning.

"I'm fine," Sue said with a sad smile.

Emily accepted the response and dropped the conversation, even though she knew deep down something was off. She didn't yet know that her mom was struggling with an addiction to alcohol and that this addiction had not only taken over her mom but her dad, too. Although Emily's parents were struggling with the impact of a disease that had nothing to do with her, she grew to believe that she was responsible for her parents' happiness and in time, everyone else's too.

During these intense arguments, Mike didn't know that Sue desperately wanted to quit drinking. He didn't realize that no matter what he did or said, Sue's inability to quit had nothing to do with him. And since Mike believed that it was his responsibility to fix his wife and have a perfect family, he continued forcing his formula for happiness onto the ones he loves most - his wife and kids.

As Mike continued to try and control his family, Emily continued to take responsibility for others' feelings. Ultimately, as the father and daughter continued to place their happiness in things outside of themselves, they both suffered.

DAD'S PERSPECTIVE ON SUFFERING

Early on in our marriage, Sue and I agreed that our children were our priority. We followed "the formula" throughout the week and by the time the weekend came, we rewarded our hard work with activities that revolved around drinking and hanging out with friends.

Over time I noticed that Sue's drinking not only increased in frequency and volume, but that she also began to drink during the week. After a long day at the office, I'd often come home to Sue drunk, something I viewed at the time as a choice, and therefore something I just couldn't understand. We had four children ranging in age from eight to fourteen years old with lots of activities to get to. I constantly wondered how she could choose to drink so much when our children needed good role models - *didn't she know they needed good role models?!*

I see now that underneath my confusion, I was also afraid. I often worried about what would happen if anyone in our small community found out about Sue's drinking problem. *What would they think? How would their judgment affect our children?*

As Sue's drinking continued to take her over, I felt increasingly resentful. In time, my wife's addiction to alcohol was met by my own addiction to control. When we were in the midst of hellacious arguments, we were completely unaware that our children could hear us. The truth is, when both of our addictions were in full swing, anyone on our little idyllic cul-de-sac could have heard us.

"Don't you want to be a good mom?" I'd often yell at Sue in an attempt to get her to stop drinking. Because I knew it was the thing she wanted most in life - to be a good mom - I thought if I could get her to see that her behavior was getting in the way of her goal, she would stop.

When my verbal attacks didn't work, I attempted to buy her sobriety with a surprise

Jeep Wrangler for her 40th birthday. When that didn't work, I tried various other forms of control and "fixing," including all the classic codependent behaviors from looking for hidden bottles of vodka, to being hyper-aware of her every move (and non-verbal signs she might be drinking), to coaching and praising and over-affirming her, and picking up the pieces if an issue arose as a result of her drinking.

Regardless of the strategy, nothing ever worked. Over time the inability to control my wife's addiction turned into rage. At times I was so consumed with anger that I threw things like dishes and laptops (always at walls and floors, never people), and I slammed doors with such force that the doorframes shattered. I see now that I resorted to this behavior because I was desperate for Sue to see how distressed I was. I believed that if she saw the pain I was in, then surely she would stop drinking. But it didn't work. Nothing I did ever worked.

At the time, I couldn't see that my own addiction to control was causing just as much damage to myself and my family as my wife's alcoholism. Looking back, I see that the more I looked outside of myself for happiness - by trying to change or manipulate people and situations in order to feel or look better - the greater my suffering.

After ten years of feeling out of control and trying to perfect everything and everyone around me, I was angry, depressed, and consumed by hopelessness. As I continued to displace my pain onto others around me, I suffered emotionally, physically, mentally, and spiritually for the following eight years as I spiraled into my own self-created hell; the only kind of hell - as far as I'm concerned - there ever really is.

Emily's Perspective on Suffering

My mom is one of the most kindhearted, loving, and understanding people I've ever known. Despite her suffering, she has always been the kind of mom and person I aspire to be: one who has always been actively engaged in my life and activities, who coached me and my siblings, and who has always been encouraging and playful. My mom is the kind of mom who unconditionally cares for, supports, and loves not just her family but anyone she meets.

As a kid, while I heard my parents argue, I never saw my mom doing anything that would indicate she had a drinking problem. I had no idea what they were arguing about. Therefore, left to my own devices to try and make sense of their arguments, I concluded there was something I could do to make it all better. In a way, my kid brain made sense of my parents' arguments like this: It was my fault if things weren't good, so I was responsible for making it (and them) better.

As I assumed responsibility for my parents' feelings, I also took on the belief that hiding my pain and sadness was the "strong" thing to do. I acquired this belief early on when I asked my mom if she was okay when she cried. She often responded through tears with: "I'm okay, Em. I'm just tired."

Despite the fact that my mom's explanation for her tears contradicted what I felt - that something more was wrong with her than just feeling tired - I still wanted to be just like my mom. I made sense of these exchanges by viewing my mom as "tough," despite her visible sadness. In time, I integrated this way of being into how I dealt with my own emotions.

By the time I was 15, I prided myself on not letting anyone see me cry. This need to be "tough," was fueled by the unconscious belief that *if I told them how I really felt, they'd feel uncomfortable and it would be my fault.*

For years I continued living like this - worrying more about making other people happy than acknowledging my own feelings. I believed that if people saw me unhappy, they would think I had no reason to feel this way. So I lived by the unconscious motto: *suppress and smile.* It didn't really matter if on the inside I was suffering, all I cared about at the time was looking "fine" on the outside. Any inquiry into how I was doing was always met with a smile and the same response I had learned growing up: "Oh yeah, I'm totally fine. I'm just tired."

Ironically, despite my valiant effort to keep everything bottled up, I desperately wanted to be heard and seen. At the same time, I had a hard time believing that if I was heard, anyone would understand how I felt. So I continued suppressing what I perceived to be "weak" emotions. As I did this, my unexpressed sadness led to undiagnosed depression and yet another reality I'd ultimately try to push down.

This pattern - and the depression - continued into my twenties. I pretended everything was okay, taking responsibility for other people's happiness while ignoring my own emotions. Eventually there was no room for me - or my needs - anywhere. For as long as I suppressed my feelings and denied the reality that I was depressed and in pain, I continued to suffer.

Surrender

"It took a long time, but I finally realized that surrender does not mean submission - it means I'm willing to stop fighting reality, to stop trying to do God's part, and to do my own."

-Courage to Change

An Unexpected Call to Face it All

Because the point at which one comes to surrender is so deeply personal, and what we believe to be a process often orchestrated by Something Else outside of the explainable, there is not one point in time when we experienced a moment of surrender concurrently. There is however an event - an experience in both of our lives - where there was a very distinct before and after that ultimately led us at different times and in different ways to the beginnings of surrender. Here is that moment in time...

In 2007, when Sue was in rehab after a relapse, Mike took Emily and her brother Matt to see a matinee. It was Matt's 18th birthday.

Twenty minutes into the movie, Mike was munching on popcorn when his cell phone started blinking. When he showed Emily and Matt the number, they instantly recognized the rehab facility their mom was at in

Cleveland. Mike told Emily and Matt to stay put while he left the theatre to take the call.

Like the obedient adult children they were, they waited patiently for their dad to return. Over an hour later, he was still nowhere in sight. Eventually, the credits rolled and the lights came on.

Without saying a word, Emily and Matt headed out of the theatre, eyes squinting as they walked quietly into the daylight, scanning the parking lot for their dad.

When they reached Mike's car, they noticed he was still on the phone, his head leaning on the steering wheel. Knowing never to disturb their dad while he was on a call, Matt and Emily sat on the curb, quietly waiting for permission to get in the car.

A few minutes later, Mike waved Emily and Matt over. He was overwhelmed with emotion and unable to filter the news he'd just received from his wife's therapist: that Sue had experienced severe childhood trauma. If she didn't address her trauma, she would continue to self-medicate and remain in active addiction.

From the back seat, Emily watched her dad wipe away tears with a lump in her throat. She felt sad, but her tears were frozen. She told herself she wasn't going to cry; she needed to be strong for her brother and her dad.

Later that day, Mike came face-to-face with a reality that brought him to his knees for the first time in his life. No matter how hard he tried to make Sue happy or sober, he didn't have the power to do so.

DAD'S PERSPECTIVE ON SURRENDER

Two weeks after that call from the rehab center, at the advice of my wife's therapy team, I entered a week-long intensive program at a retreat center in Tennessee. I needed to address the effects of the secondary PTSD I was experiencing, as well as begin to learn about my own addictions to codependency and anger.

While I can't prove it, I believe that entering the retreat center 14 years ago was God gracefully shoving me into the abyss of letting go (even though I wouldn't have called it that back then). But it wasn't like everything changed for the better right away just because I sought help. In fact, it initially seemed like things got worse before they got better. Because I was no longer running from the pain - and was now facing it head-on - I had no choice but to begin letting go of "the formula." I found myself face-to-face with the twelve years of repressed anger that I'd bottled up. It needed to be expressed and released.

This initial experience of surrender was a felt sense of powerlessness for me. It was in this powerlessness that I blamed God for my wife's trauma and addiction and for my children's pain. I blamed God for all pain.

While in Tennessee, I learned that a significant number of children (and far too many) - both boys and girls - experience trauma before the age of eighteen. As I learned more about the reality and prevalence of trauma and pain, my world was turned upside down. Despite being a devout Catholic my entire life, I began to question if there ever even was a God.[3]

I found myself rejecting the notion that God could protect me and my family. I began to believe that it no longer mattered if I was good and did what was right, because if God was real in the first place, he wouldn't have allowed so many people to suffer.

At some point, I gave up on God. For many months, my relationship with Him/Her was limited to a simple, but repetitive statement: "F*@% you, God."

I believe that the process of surrender is unique to each individual. The choice to embark on my own healing was the beginning of this process for me. It was also the point at which I accepted that I was not responsible for my loved ones' happiness - I was only responsible for my own. In time I learned that this responsibility meant facing all the unhappy things in my life, including how I'd turned my back on God.

Today I see that despite all of my blame, anger, hatred, and condemnation of God, God never flinched. In fact, She was embracing me with Infinite Love, allowing me to have whatever feelings I needed to work through during (and still today) each moment of surrender.

As a result of receiving this infinite love and mercy, surrender has evolved into a daily (and at times, moment-to-moment) genuflecting to the mystery of life, just as it is. Through the Grace of suffering and surrender, in time I have come to embrace the freedom of the present moment for whatever this may be - a process that has and will continue to take years of practice and prayer.

Emily's Perspective on Surrender

As we drove home from the theatre that day, I felt frozen with shock. At 20 years old, my heart shattered as I watched my dad cry and listened to him share the news about my mom. I too wanted to cry, but the intensity of the shock (and my need to be "strong") blocked me from experiencing any tears.

How could this happen, I wondered? My mom is the most amazing person in the world. How could God let all of this happen to her? I was still in denial. My mom, an alcoholic? No way. Trauma? Absolutely not. My family is perfect, this can't be real.

But my denial and questions didn't change the truth, the pain, or the reality that I no longer had a "normal" family.

Our cultural conditioning often teaches us that we have to be upbeat, happy, and positive - to put on a smile - even when we're in pain. This need to be upbeat and gloss over my pain led me to a need for busyness that wouldn't let me slow down. For the next three years, because of how I learned to cope with my emotions, I decided it was best for me to not discuss any of my feelings and instead continue to go through the motions, living life with a business-as-usual attitude.

"Em, just sit with me for a second," my roommate pleaded with me one day while I was in college. "I have not talked to you all week, you're always just go-go-go. You have to stop."

But I couldn't stop. I didn't know what to do with any of the feelings or thoughts I was having. It felt as though I was in a dark cloud of pain that had to constantly be pushed down. I feared that if I slowed down - or stopped to look at the pain - that dark cloud would take me over.

Despite holding up an *everything-is-fine* facade, I was very aware that I was struggling on the inside. Then, during one particular trip to visit my mom in rehab, I learned the serenity prayer: *God, Grant me the serenity to accept the things I cannot change, the courage to change the things I can, and the wisdom to know the difference.*

This prayer became my desperate plea for help each night as I lay in my bed and quietly sobbed, just as I did when I was a little girl. On some nights I said it over and over again, often leaving out "God" at the beginning because at that point, I wasn't quite sure He was with me or could even hear me.

A year later on September 14, 2008, while studying in Puebla, Mexico for the semester, I experienced another life event that led me to call on The Serenity Prayer.

While with some friends on a weekend trip in Oaxaca, I came in from a long day at the beach and looked at my phone. I noted several calls and text messages, many saying "I'm sorry, Em." When I came across a text that said: "Em, you need to call your dad," my heart began to race.

My dad told me that my dear friend, Michael, had died by suicide the day before. My knees buckled as I fell to the ground. My body couldn't handle the news. I sat in my hut and sobbed for hours.

Over the next two years, I unconsciously continued to live my life in a downward, silent spiral, filled with pain and suffering. As the sadness I'd been carrying around for years intensified with the loss of my friend, I was eventually diagnosed with clinical depression.

In July of 2010, three years after that matinee at the theatre, I felt like there was no escape from my pain. This was rock bottom. I gave up on fighting the dark cloud and hiding my suffering. No one, not even my family knew the extent of my pain, and I couldn't pretend I was fine for one more day. I knew I could no longer go it alone, so I finally told my family the truth about how I felt. I then spent a few days in a treatment center where I began to honestly address my painful emotions.

While this was the ultimate lowest point in my life, it was also a turning point. I felt that I had somehow given my pain over to Something Else. As a result, I began to experience more compassion for myself. I saw that what I had been through was a lot of shit for one person to endure, and all before I had reached 23 years old. Most importantly, opening up to the loving support around me showed me that I no longer had to hide the pain.

As I began to accept the reality of what I'd been through (and the emotions that came along with this reality), I also began to experience the first underpinnings of surrender in my life. I discovered that I didn't have to *like* what I'd been through or even be okay with it. I saw that now I could choose how I responded to life. As a result, I began to shift out of going-through-the-motions mode and into living life with more self-awareness.

One month after my first true experience of surrender, the universe dropped an unexpected and unsolicited opportunity into my lap: to work as an au pair in Milan, Italy. Because I was so clear that I wanted to fully live my life and enjoy all that this world has to offer, I jumped at the opportunity to leave the country for a new adventure. It was this adventure that opened me up to a practice that ultimately changed my life for the better.

Practice

Dad! Don't Throw Your Gum Out the Window!

We discovered the following Four-Step Exercise in 2011 when we began studying the work of Anthony deMello (1932-1988). The recordings of his "Wake Up To Life" conference were particularly transformative for us. This practice has transformed all of our relationships, including our father-daughter relationship:

1. Notice the negative feeling.

2. Understand that the feeling is in you - *no event or circumstance has the power to cause you to feel anyway.*

3. Never identify with that feeling.

4. Understand that when you change, everything changes.

In the fall of 2011, Mike and Emily pulled into the local high school to watch a family member's soccer match. As Mike searched for a spot to park, the cool, fall breeze blew through the rolled-down windows of the car. Without a thought, Mike wadded up his stale gum and threw it out the window.

"Dad! Don't throw your gum out the window!" Emily called out.

Mike looked over at Emily with a puzzled face, shocked that his normally mild-mannered 24-year-old daughter was now telling him what to do.

In response to the perplexed look on her dad's face, Emily provided some justification for her command: "Gum pollution is on the rise. And, don't you know a bird could die from it?"

Completely out of character, Mike stopped the car, opened the door, grabbed the gum wrapper, and searched for the gum on the ground. He found it by a drain, picked it up, then wrapped it in paper so he could toss it in a garbage can later.

While they didn't speak of the incident any further that day, both Emily and Mike were quietly surprised by it. Emily couldn't believe that she could speak so freely to her dad without receiving a lecture in return. Mike couldn't believe that he had actually picked up the gum.

Years later when Emily and Mike decided to write this book together, they reflected on how the gum incident signified a turning point in their relationship. They realized it was (and continues to be) their commitment to a daily practice - in particular the Four-Step Exercise - that allowed them to relate in a new way; a way that created space for Emily to speak her truth and for Mike to listen.

DAD'S PERSPECTIVE ON PRACTICE

"I hope I'm going to be wise here and make no attempt whatsoever to wake you up if you are asleep. It is really none of my business, even though I say to you at times, 'wake up!' My business is to do my thing, to dance my dance. If you profit from it, fine; if you don't, too bad!"

-Anthony deMello[4]

These were some of the first words I heard from TDM when I began listening to his CD series in 2011. I experienced deMello's voice as light-hearted and unattached to his message. I also noted a sense of freedom when he spoke. He didn't seem to give a damn. Because at the time I was still so addicted to thinking I could change those around me and desperately wanted to feel free, I was very drawn to TDM's nonattachment. I wanted what he had.

Tony deMello's message about awareness drew me in even more. He was a Catholic priest, but I'd never heard a priest discuss ideas like this -- awareness is love, spirituality is about unlearning, or that it's infinitely more important to question your beliefs than to just swallow them whole.[5] These messages sparked my curiosity and had me consistently coming back for more.

In time I realized that the more I listened to deMello's teachings, the more I felt called to apply them to my life. When he introduced the Four-Step Exercise, I felt particularly intrigued by his comment: "Try this a thousand times and you'll be amazed at what happens, but most of you won't. Most people don't want to change."[6]

Because I've always been up for a good challenge - especially when someone suggests I can't meet said challenge - deMello's statement fueled a part of me that wanted to prove him wrong. When I committed to the practice, ultimately it didn't matter how I got there. What mattered was that I had arrived.

As a result of stepping into the practice, I experienced many unanticipated challenges. By the grace of God, however, I remained committed and began to question everything. In time I noticed that I was beginning to see things differently.

As TDM says, "We see people and things not as they are, but as we are."[7] As I became more open to new ways of being, my previous formula for success was shaken to its core. At the same time, I also began to experience positive shifts, particularly while driving in the car.

At some point while driving, I noticed that instead of habitually reacting to other drivers on the road (whom I deemed to have poor driving skills) and directing my anger onto them, I began to practice Step One: I simply *noticed* the anger that arose in my body.

As I noticed the anger, I then went to Step Two and repeated deMello's words to myself:

no event or circumstance has the power to cause me to feel any particular way.

Gradually, I began to smile and laugh at the anger (or what I would have labeled "frustration" at the time). I began to see that when I observed the anger, I was able to catch the energy, let it go, and no longer identify with it.

When I extended the practice of noticing my anger to other situations - like with my kids, an employee, my wife, my dad, or even a customer service rep - I repeated to myself: *no event or circumstance or person can cause me to feel any particular way.*

After Steps One and Two, Step Three showed me that who I truly am is not the anger. Instead, I am simply experiencing the feeling of anger. Because I felt justified in responding with anger for so much of my life, this disidentification helped me to let go of trying to control life and allow peace to arise from within me.

As for Step Four, I really had no idea what "when you change, everything and everyone changes" meant. I was so conditioned to believe that my happiness was dependent on external circumstances, people, and things, that it took time for me to fully understand that this step is actually the beneficial result of practicing the first three steps.

What I did gain from Step Four, within my first few years of practice, was a glimmer of hope that maybe I could be freed from feeling responsible for changing those around me. As the inner resonance of this step grew stronger, I came to realize that the only thing I can change is myself. As a result, this practice of not identifying with my feelings, habits, and patterns has led to transformations in all of my relationships, and in particular with my daughter, Emily.

By the time the gum conversation with Emily came about, I'd been practicing a lot of self-observation, something that I didn't even know existed prior to listening to Tony deMello. Had the incident occurred a few years earlier, I would have most likely met Emily's request to pick up the gum with resentment and anger, followed by an I'm-the-dad- you-do-not-tell-me-what-to-do type of lecture.

Today I sense that what seems like such a trivial event - *a daughter telling her dad to not throw his gum out the window* - was in fact a very significant turning point in my relationship with Emily. According to my daughter, it was at this point that she felt she could speak openly and from her heart without any fear of retaliation from me.

It is with a commitment to practice, trusting in the process of this practice, and having faith in life itself, that these types of subtle interactions and events in our everyday lives provide the opportunity to choose a different way. Because the way we do anything is the way we do everything (as Richard Rohr often says), this process has not only helped me to be a more peaceful and conscious driver and experience a new relationship with my daughter, it has also transformed (and continues to transform) how I am being and doing (and thus experiencing) everything.

Emily's Perspective on Practice

As I was adjusting to life in Milan and experiencing positive shifts in my life that I hoped would stick, I decided listening to some positive words on the daily might help. I searched "happiness" on Apple Podcasts and came across Gary van Warmerdam's The Pathway to Happiness. He spoke about things like the "four agreements" and "dismantling your belief systems." Because I didn't understand what he was saying, I found myself going back to listen again and again. This process of returning to Gary's podcast almost every day became my very first experience of a daily practice.

Then one day while I was on a Skype call with my dad he shared about a teacher he was listening to named Tony deMello. I noticed how energized he was while talking about TDM and I also felt intrigued when he mentioned terms that I had heard from the Pathway to Happiness podcast.

A few months later when I returned to Cincinnati, my daily practice shifted from listening to Gary every day to listening to TDM's CDs and practicing the Four-Step exercise. As I grew and evolved, so did my practice.

I enjoyed listening to Tony, and I began to notice more shifts - like the one with the gum incident - in my conversations with my dad. As I continued to experience these subtle changes within myself, I wanted more. In time as I continued to practice the Four-Step Exercise and experienced positive shifts in my life, I learned to trust in this newfound process.

Similar to my dad, I first began practicing Step One - noticing the feeling - while driving. If I drove behind someone who "didn't know how to drive," I began to notice - and honestly, laugh at myself - as my hands gripped the steering wheel and I yelled at the driver in front of me to "LEARN HOW TO FLIPPING DRIVE!"

As these brief moments of *noticing the feeling* happened more frequently, they eventually revealed a major pattern in my relationships: that I felt responsible for other people's feelings, and that I judged them when they didn't do what I thought was *right*. These revelations also reiterated what I'd been learning about surrender: that the only thing I can control is myself, and that I am responsible for how I am being in the world. Embracing this understanding is Step Two.

I recognized the Step Two experience as my dad walked me out to my car after spending the day by the pool at my parents' house one Sunday evening. After he made a comment and I replied with one of my typical sarcastic responses, he simply and lovingly said: "Em, enough with the sarcasm, okay? It hurts."

This exchange took me by surprise because my dad typically responded to my sarcasm with an angry lecture about how I shouldn't talk to him that way. But this time, his energy was calm and loving, and it hit me in a new way.

As I got into my car and drove away, tears streamed down my face. I couldn't believe what my dad had said. *I thought I was just being funny? I mean, I am hilarious. How did I have the power to hurt my dad? He's the dad. I can't do that. He's the one that's in control?*

My dad's reaction to my sarcasm was Step Four in action: when we change, everyone and everything changes.

For the next few weeks, I continued to reflect on my dad's words and his energy: *Enough with the sarcasm, okay Em? It hurts.* In time I realized that this experience had more to do with me - and how the sadness I felt deep down was coming out sideways in the form of sarcasm - than it had to do with my dad or our relationship.

At some point after this interaction, while driving along in my Jetta, I heard Tony say: "You step outside of yourself and look at that depression, and don't identify with it. You don't do a thing to make it go away; you are perfectly willing to go on with your life while it passes through you and disappears."[8]

It was as if a wave of relief rushed over me. I was finally able to let go of identifying with my sadness and embody the notion that I am not my depression. That was my Step Three.

Ultimately the Four-Step Exercise allowed me to step outside of myself and observe my experience as if it was happening to someone else. As a result, I finally began to break free from being Emily, a depressed, sad person, into Emily, a person who was experiencing depression and sadness.

Self-Awareness

"There is nothing more important than awareness... what you are aware of you are in control of, what you are not aware of, controls you"

-Tony deMello

What Pushes Our Buttons

"Em, I've asked you to please put the remote back," Mike said calmly to twenty-six-year-old Emily, who sat on the couch across from him. "Can you help me find it?"

At the sound of the word "remote," Emily instinctively began to daze out. She knew this scenario all too well and wasn't in the mood to feel wronged today. Emily knew that inevitably after she did something "wrong" - in this case, losing the remote - she'd receive a long-winded lecture on how she *should* have done it differently (like put the remote back in its place or just not have taken it from its place at all).

Mike watched as Emily eventually scrambled to try and find the remote. He thought back to all the times over the years she (or one of his other kids) had misplaced the remote and not returned it to its "proper" place. He remembered how this had always been such a conundrum for him.

"It's simple, just put the damn remote back in its place!" he'd often think to himself and inevitably demand of his kids.

But this time, Mike wasn't so bothered by the missing remote. He felt calmer. He was watching his tone and his energy, and he knew he was just making a simple request of his daughter.

Emily, on the other hand, hadn't yet noticed her dad's calm energy. She still anticipated a lecture and thus got lost in defensive thoughts: *I'm twenty-six years old and still getting lectures from my dad. Why does he continue to treat me like a child?*

"Can you think where you might have had it last, Em?" Her dad asked with a helpful, inquisitive tone.

As Mike continued to offer his help, Emily noticed something different compared to previous times when she'd lost the remote. There was no aggressive finger pointing, no belittling, no eyebrows raised in disappointment, no judgment, no air that he was right and she was wrong. There wasn't even a hint of resentful energy in the air. Instead, he spoke with soft words and a calm voice.

Emily realized her dad's harsh finger point had now somehow softened into a hand gesture that suggested a tone of love and respect, rather than anger and condescension. After years of lectures and feeling wronged, Emily realized she could now actually hear her dad's request, and somehow she didn't feel a need to throw an all-too-familiar sarcastic dagger in defense.

A few minutes later, Emily found the remote under one of the seat cushions and simply handed it to her dad.

DAD'S PERSPECTIVE ON SELF-AWARENESS

Prior to becoming more self-aware, my pattern of thought - with regard to a lost remote - would've looked like this: *Everyone knows the remote control should be placed on the coffee table when done using it. This is simple to do! How could this be so damn complicated for someone to understand?! Just put the damn remote back in its place.*

When my expectations weren't met, my pattern of behavior often included a downpour of resentment onto whomever was not doing whatever thing as perfectly as I thought it should be done. In certain incidents - like the one with Emily and the remote - I am now fairly certain that while I didn't outright say this, my underlying message really said: *what the hell is wrong with you, Em?*

Despite several years of consistent meditation practice, as well as practicing Tony's Four-Step Exercise, I knew I needed more inner work. I wanted to take a deeper dive into better understanding myself and how I operated. When I began to notice shifts with my son, Matt, I got curious about what had contributed to those shifts. I learned that he'd been studying the Enneagram at the School for Conscious Living in Cincinnati (SCL).[9] That sparked my interest. Soon after discovering the Enneagram, I enrolled in Deborah Ooten's two-year program on the Enneagram and Spiral Dynamics at SCL. I have been using both these tools in all aspects of my life since beginning the course.

Early on in my studies at SCL, I discovered that I am a Type One personality (aka "The Perfectionist", "The Judge" or "The Reformer"). I learned that my shadow self - which for me is expressed mainly through resentment, anger, and perfectionism - can be at play without my awareness. Furthermore, I learned that I unconsciously believed that I was a failure if I wasn't perfect - especially in my role as a dad - and thus, I extended this expectation for perfection to the rest of my family. Because I unconsciously resented anyone whose behavior led me to feeling like a failure, for many years at any given time, I had a well of anger ready to explode if anyone - especially my children - did not do something as perfectly as I thought it should be done.

I also learned through the Enneagram that my personality patterns had taken hold by the time I was seven years old, so the way my personality had developed was not my fault, nor was it anyone else's fault. As a result, I was finally able to see my behaviors as separate from my true self. I saw that my resentment, anger, and perfectionism were actually products of how the little boy in me emotionally responded to living in an imperfect world, not reflections of who I really am. This understanding allowed me to begin to hold compassion for myself and my experience, and in time I learned to accept and embrace my undesirable behaviors with grace and my positive attributes with humility.

As I began to learn more about my fixation on perfection, I saw how it led me to try to control everything with my kids - from school, to sports, to relationships, and even to how they handled using the remote control. Today I can see how this fixation translated into an angry, judgemental response to a misplaced remote: because Emily couldn't put the remote back where it needed to go - which I viewed as imperfection - and because she was my child, I unconsciously believed she would be a failure in the world, and thus, I was a failure as a dad.

Slowly, as I learned how to embrace all of me - even the most undesirable aspects of my personality - I became less judgemental of myself and others. The reactivity that previously would have lasted for days or weeks no longer has such a hold on me. As a result, and with grace, more freedom for my true self continues to emerge.

As I continued to release unhealthy patterns of reacting, I became increasingly aware that it was not only me doing the letting go, but that Something Greater was also at play (more on this in the next chapter). As a result, what would have once been a critical response toward my daughter for losing the remote, now became a space for a loving and kind exchange.

As Carl Jung said, "One does not become enlightened by imagining figures of light, but by making the darkness conscious."[10] Becoming self-aware has helped me to shine a light on the more hidden, "darker" aspects of my personality that (when they remain unconscious) lead to thoughts and behaviors that disrupt my connection to God, to myself, to my family, and to the world. Today I embrace these undesirable parts of myself with gratitude because I see that they aren't flaws I have to be ashamed of or deny; they are all a part of me that lead to serenity when I embrace them.

Looking back, I can see my dad's unconscious belief (that his worth as a dad relied on my "good" behavior), manifested in the unconscious belief I held throughout my childhood that I was "bad" if I made a mistake. At some point, making a mistake not only meant that I was bad, but also that I just couldn't do things right - like put the remote back in its place. This belief accompanied me into adulthood, showing up in various situations, including while I was at work.

In my second year as a first-grade teacher, during a lecture about how leaves change color in the fall, I noticed I had typed "chlorophyl" instead of "chlorophyll" on a presentation I was sharing with my kiddos. Immediately after I noticed the error, I remembered that I'd sent the powerpoint out to the other teachers. As I imagined my colleagues seeing my mistake, a rush of shame flooded my body. Because I believed that I was not a good teacher if I made a mistake, I assumed my peers would also think I wasn't a good teacher. I felt paralyzed by my fear of judgment and fumbled through the rest of the lesson.

In retrospect I can see that the heightened emotion I experienced that day to something so minor was an indication that my emotional experience wasn't really about the missing "L," it was about something deeper: how I felt in response to an old belief that I could never do anything right.

At the time, however, there was no way you could have convinced me this situation was about anything other than the missing "L." It really looked like the spelling error was the problem! So in order to solve this massive "problem" (aka try and get rid of my uncomfortable feelings), I stopped mid-lecture to correct the spelling of chlorophyll - even though my audience was a bunch of seven-year-olds who may have never heard of this word, much less know how to spell it.

Because our programming becomes so unconsciously ingrained into every part of our being, it often looks like the truth. This can make the path of awareness challenging, because we are going against years of experiences we've unconsciously gathered in our artillery as evidence to support our beliefs as facts (i.e. - I lost the remote again, so of course I can't do anything right).

Without giving ourselves permission to get curious about and begin to question how and why we operate the way we do, we risk getting stuck in our programming. We risk getting stuck in the egoic part of ourselves that thinks we're "not a good teacher" because we spelled chlorophyll wrong. Lacking awareness of how our unconscious beliefs play out in our daily lives blocks us from experiencing who we truly are. Awareness not only helps us to understand and name why and how we're operating the way we are - more importantly, it also shows us where we're operating *from* when we're operating from our programming versus our essence.

With relationships, when two people are unaware of their unconscious beliefs, we often see a similar pattern to the missing "L" incident. Without awareness of what's happening under the surface with each person, it often looks like the "problem" is the missing "L". Bringing the unconscious to the conscious in every interaction allows us to choose to step outside of ourselves, breathe, and see that the intensity of the situation isn't necessarily about the missing "L,"it's about how we are all just trying to navigate through our unconscious beliefs and uncomfortable feelings.

Without awareness, our own unconscious beliefs, thoughts, and patterns (disguised as "problems") threaten to keep us asleep. As we choose to step outside of ourselves during heated experiences, we begin to wake up from the same old unconscious song and dance in our relationships. This process of becoming more aware allows us to let go and see that the thing isn't really about the thing.

Letting Go

"Alternative consciousness is largely letting go of my mind's need to solve problems, to fix people, to fix myself, to rearrange the moment because it is not to my liking. When that mind goes, another, the non-dualistic mind is already there waiting. We realize it is actually our natural way of seeing. It's the way we thought as children before we started judging and analyzing and distinguishing things one from another."

- Richard Rohr

When Resentment Bubbles Up

"Wait, what time are we all meeting tonight?" Emily was just a tad frantic.

"We rescheduled for 6:30 - 7:30, remember? I sent that text a couple days ago," Mike responded.

By the fall of 2020, Mike and Emily had a good groove for the weekly meetings when they got together to work on their book. They met for two hours in the evening on Wednesdays, with 5:30-6:30 devoted to working with Mike's eldest daughter and Emily's sister, Sarah, who was also their writing coach.

On this particular week, however, Emily forgot they had changed their meeting time. Her heart sank when she realized she had scheduled a meeting with a colleague during the same time they planned to meet with Sarah.

"It's okay, Em," Mike said lovingly. "You can just hop off the call when you need to hop off."

For a moment, Emily dazed out as she listened to the familiar voice of her inner critic chattering away about her irresponsibility in messing up her schedule for the second time this week. In addition to the negative self-talk, she noticed a bit of defensiveness rising in her.

Just as quickly as her negative thoughts jumped in, however, so did her awareness that these were just thoughts, they were not necessarily the truth about who she really was. Furthermore, her dad's calm energy reminded her that she now had the ability to choose her response and return to the present moment.

Emily asked for a second to breathe so she could get herself present.

After a minute or so of silence and as Emily finally let go of her negative self-talk, a loud burp erupted from her mouth.

"Ope, excuse me!" Emily said with an innocent giggle. "It's the seltzer water I'm drinking! It gives me the seltzer burps!"

Mike responded with silence. Within a nanosecond, he noticed a tinge of resentful energy emerge in his body. He watched as the resentment spurred thoughts of how others need to get control of themselves. He also wondered why Emily didn't just review her text messages to clarify the time?

In the next second, though, Mike noticed the negative nature of his thoughts and feelings and realized he was simply triggered. Instead of getting swept away by his thoughts or instinctively reacting to his emotions, he was able to embrace the negative energy within him and get present. Because he now knew that Something Greater would help him to let go, his reactivity faded just as quickly as it had bubbled up.

After both of their internal shifts, despite the glitch in the length of time of the call, Emily and Mike connected on a deep level and proceeded to have a productive conversation.

During their next writing session a few days later, Mike and Emily shared their inner experiences from the call with the burp. Exploring the reactive thoughts and feelings they had experienced reminded them of a time when Emily was in fifth grade and needed help with her homework. Mike recalled how he sat with eleven-year-old Emily at the computer, lecturing her about how she needed to stop hiccuping when he was trying to help her. Emily recalled wondering how the hell she was going to stop hiccuping, meanwhile internalizing that somehow she was wrong for having the hiccups in the first place.

The two laughed as they realized how the same intense thoughts and feelings from their programming could still easily arise in them today, twenty-five years later. For Mike, the uncontrollable nature of a seltzer burp can still strike the same chord as a hiccup once did. For Emily, the inner dialogue of "messing up" can still come on just as strong today as it did as a kid in the face of a "mistake." Small as it may seem, though, the two realized that it is these types of changes that have led to the inner shifts that continue to unlock the doorways into the larger opportunities to let go.

DAD'S PERSPECTIVE ON LETTING GO

Reflecting on the judgmental reactions I had with Emily when she was in fifth grade is so damn humbling. I can't help but look at my younger self and wonder: *how in the world could I have reacted so negatively to a child's hiccup?*

I now see that this response was my unconscious programming of control and perfection, something that has nothing to do with Emily and everything to do with my experience of being human. Today, instead of getting hung up on these past mistakes, I now choose to make amends for how I've behaved and then ask for forgiveness when necessary. I accept that at any given time I am always doing my best, that I will continue to make mistakes, and that it's best to simply acknowledge my part and move forward.

Becoming more conscious of my patterns of reacting has allowed me to see that my habitual responses don't just miraculously disappear. In fact, as evidenced by my inner experience with Emily's burp – twenty-five years later - it's clear that many of these patterns are still here.

After years of practice and inner work, it is humbling to see how in a nanosecond I can be flooded with judgment, resentment, anger, and criticism of myself and others. Having an understanding, though, that these negative emotions are part of the human experience and part of who I am, has allowed me to embrace all of me. As a result, I am now able to extend the same acceptance to others.

While I'm not happy about the damage my resentment and anger have caused, it is as liberating as it is humbling to accept that they are parts of me that I no longer have to deny. Acknowledging that they happen allows me to let go of them more easily when they do arise. Over time, this experience of recognizing negative energy, catching it in the moment, embracing it, and then allowing myself to let go with Something Greater has led to deeper levels of peace and serenity in my life.

But how do we begin to go about learning to let go? Well, we practice.

For some people, while letting go of habitual patterns of reacting may happen overnight, for most of us - myself included - it takes time and years of practice -- practice that I imagine will last a lifetime.

In my experience, letting go doesn't have to be limited to only one practice. There are many practices that can aid us in learning to let go. Over the years I have tried several, including Zen meditation, which was recommended by my cardiologist at a time when it felt like my heart was going to beat out of my chest from stress. It helped me re-learn how to breathe, and it continues to help when I choose to drop into this practice from time to time.

Other practices I have embraced since I first encountered TDM's Four Step Exercise include Lectio Divina[11] as well as a guided meditation by Dr. Deborah Ooten and Ron Esposito called Lifting the Veil: A Guide to Meditation and Letting Go of the Six Objects of Attention.[12] I currently still work with both of these practices from time to time.

Centering prayer[13], which I learned through studying with Cynthia Bourgeault and reading her book: *Centering Prayer and Inner Awakening*[14], has become the cornerstone of my ability to let go. It is the most consistent practice I have worked with to this day.

While these practices have been the most useful for me, I don't believe they're the only methods that aid in letting go. In fact, it's my opinion that the type of practice we choose is not nearly as important as our commitment to staying with it.

If you want to learn how to let go, my advice is to find a practice that speaks most directly to your heart and then stick with it. In time you will find that "if you stay faithful to your practice, your practice will stay faithful to you."[15]

For me, the ability to let go has opened up doors in my life that I didn't even know were possible to open. In particular, it has given me the opportunity to bring new eyes, fresh ears, a non-judging mind, and an open heart into my relationship with my daughter. It has led to deeply meaningful conversations. Letting go has carved out space for a deeper connection that allows me to see Emily as a unique individual on her own path in life.

Ultimately, letting go has freed me from the type of parenting that previously resulted in pushing achievement and success and criticism when things weren't the way I thought they should be. It has allowed me to become a dad who is free amidst both the "good" and "bad" of life. At the end of the day, the biggest miracle resulting from letting go has simply been the ability to be present with not only my daughter and who she is, but accepting all of life and all that is.

88

Emily's Perspective on Letting Go

During the call with my dad when I made the mistake of double booking, I was instantly aware of the old stories about looming self-annihilation that often play out in my head when I make mistakes like this. The stories typically go something like this: *I did it again, I'm always doing the wrong thing. I am so unreliable. I just wish I could do the right thing.*

However, after years of self-observation and learning to dis-identify with negative thoughts and feelings, coupled with the knowledge that I was in a supportive space with my dad, I was able to first notice what I needed and then ask: "Can I just have a minute?"

Once I paused, I was then able to let go of my reactivity, close my eyes, take a deep breath in, and say: *Universe, please help me.* Followed by: *I love you, Emily. You are loved.*

With the Universe's help, I was able to witness, pause, choose a new path, and then let go of my old pattern of self-annihilation based on the belief that I was a terrible person.

But how did I get from the brink of self-annihilation to letting go? Welp, for starters, a whole heck of a lot of help from different teachers and lots of embracing all kinds of different practices. To be honest, I attribute the ability to let go to the melting pot of practices I have assimilated over the years.

But seriously, if my practices were a melting pot, it would look a bit like this: as a base ingredient, start off with Gary van Warmerdam's Pathway to Happiness podcast[16] and Tony deMello's Wake Up to Life Conference, add a little bit of Louise Hay's Mirror Work[17], throw in a dash of Robert Holden's Loveability[18] with a side of Deborah Ooten's Enneagram Emersion, dump a few scoops of Gabriel Bernstein's messages about the universe and choosing love[19], sprinkle some manifesting with Abraham Hicks[20] and a few oracle cards, and you've got my personal practice recipe for the ability to let go of old patterns and choose a new way in the face of a challenging moment. And, if you want some dessert, explore the metaphysical meaning of crystals and the spiritual meaning of animals that cross your path.

The really cool thing about this melting pot is that while the bowl - aka the framework - stays the same (meditating daily, journaling, reading spiritual work, and exercising), my personal recipe - aka the specific type of inner work I practice - is ever evolving.

I'm always welcoming new teachers and practices. When I need help letting go, any one of them may bubble up. The point is, though, while my practice is a hodgepodge of teachings and is ever evolving, as long as I am consistent with a practice, something always simmers to the top.

What happens when something simmers to the top?

Well, when I double booked myself and noticed my ego telling stories about that situation, I knew I needed to pause. I was then able to recognize I had a choice: I could continue in the same self-annihilating patterns or I could choose to love myself. Each piece of this response happened in a nano-second. This was not only a culmination of all of the teachings and practices I have learned over the years but there was also a little Higher Power Help (HPH).

The outcome is that over time I am much better able to let go of old patterns. But to be honest, I'm not really sure *how* it happens. I just know - as my dad always says - this shit works. My experience is that somewhere along the line the teachings move from a mental construction to an embodied experience and with that HPH from the universe, poof! I often find myself in a powerful shift.

For me, the ultimate lesson I continue to find myself returning to since committing to a practice of becoming more conscious and letting go is learning how to be more graceful and gentle with myself and knowing that I am perfectly imperfect. When I allow myself to see that mistakes are pointers for growth, it shifts the grace within me. This is the crux of letting go for me: it's not about achieving perfection, instead, it is through the practice of letting go that we learn to embrace the imperfections.

Whenever I am feeling comfortable about my progress, as if I have learned all that I have to learn, the universe humbles me with a new experience that takes me back to an old pattern in a nanosecond. While this is challenging and uncomfortable, guess what? It never fails to bring with it a new lesson. When I am ready to see these lessons - whether it's through my inner ten-year-old or my adult self - the lessons just keep on coming, pointing to what I need to learn, what I am ready to let go of, and how to accept what is.

Acceptance

"All is well and everything is a mess."

-Tony deMello

It Is What It Is

It was the fall of 2020. Mike and Emily had been meeting virtually to work on the book during the pandemic.

"How are you doing, dad?" Emily asked at the beginning of a book writing session.

"Feeling pretty good," Mike replied. "How are you doing today, Em?"

"I'm good!" Emily said, realizing almost immediately that this was an old I'm-fine-when-I'm-really-not type of response. "Okay, that's actually a lie."

"Do you want to talk about it or do you want to start working?" Mike asked.

"Let's just start working - I'm over it," Emily said.

Mike smiled.

"Actually, can I just tell you this?" Emily continued with a tone that indicated she clearly was not over it. "I left work today really struggling. I am feeling stressed out and frustrated with a lot of things that are happening, which has me questioning if I really am living the work we're writing about."

Mike noticed what looked and sounded like Em's familiar fear and anger. But instead of trying to make her feelings go away - like he might have tried in the past - he chose a different approach to supporting her as she moved through these feelings.

"Can I suggest that we do something, Em?" He asked.

"Yeah," Emily replied.

"Let's go back and read some of what we have already written," Mike suggested.

Emily wanted to get out of her funk, so she welcomed her dad's idea and agreed to read back through their work.

As they read the chapter on Practice Emily was reminded of Step One: to get in touch with the negative feeling. When she did, she noticed the fear and anger begin to dissipate. As she let go of resisting the feelings, and instead accepted and consciously disidentified with them, she remembered that this too, both her feelings and the challenging work situation, shall pass.

Emily shared her experience with her dad as it was unfolding for her. Mike offered his support by not interfering with her feelings or her process. He also noted an inner sense that this too shall pass and that jumping in to try to make it better would not be useful for his daughter.

As Emily continued to read, she felt herself working through her feelings of fear and self-doubt.

"I just know that I have a choice," she said with conviction. "I know that the fear and stress of this moment are temporary. I know that things will unfold the way they need to for me and everyone involved in this situation."

As Emily and her dad shifted gears into writing their chapter on Acceptance, they discussed how they both felt grateful for the reminder that the work is never over and that acceptance - of themselves, each other, and all of life in general - is always possible even when everything is a mess.

DAD'S PERSPECTIVE ON ACCEPTANCE

As Emily and I reread our chapter on practice, I noticed that while I can still go to a reactive space - even after ten years of practicing the Four-Step Exercise - by the grace of God, I just don't stay there as long. To repeat Jim Finley, something I've learned to be true is that "if you stay faithful to your practice, your practice will stay faithful to you."

When I watched Emily experience fear and anger, I noticed I had thoughts of wanting to rescue her from her emotional experience so that she could feel better. Because I was aware of my own inner experience in real time, however, I was able to let the thoughts go and I chose to not intrude on her process.

For many years prior to this, I undoubtedly would have reacted to these thoughts by trying to "fix" Emily (or the situation) or by villainizing the other by blaming them for "making" my daughter feel the way she did. These were unconscious reactions that typically reflected how I unknowingly made the situation about me. On the surface it looked like I was trying to help Emily, but the driving force beneath the behavior was my own discomfort from not being able to control the situation or make her feel better.

Today I am no longer unconsciously swept up in trying to fix things for my kids or blaming others for their problems, because I know that my value and worth as a human being is inherent, regardless of what is happening in the world around me. I also know that simply because I am human, my habitual responses can (and still do) surface in a nanosecond.

Over time, throughout many more failures than successes, I've noticed that as I slip back into anger or fear or sadness, it's as if Something Else is assisting me in observing "Mike" in the experience. Richard Rohr calls this: "the stable witness."[21]

Rohr explains that once we are in the space of the stable witness, "now [we] can laugh or weep over [our] little dramas and dances, without being attached to them or hating them. [We] can look at [ourselves] and others calmly and compassionately because [we] are able to see things as they are in themselves and not from the viewpoint of how they affect [us]."

Embracing the stable witness allows us in time to accept all of ourselves, all of life, and every moment just as it is. This idea that we don't have to *do* anything to be accepted is the opposite of how many of us are taught to go out into the world and strive, achieve, accomplish, and do "good" in order to be worthy as human beings; that we have to do and be "good" in order to be accepted by those around us and ultimately to earn God's acceptance. This is an illusion, however, because true acceptance is not something we have to earn, it is something that is innately given. It is a gift; a gift that has already and always will be given.

Over time, as I have learned how to accept all of myself, including my failures, sins, righteousness, judgmentalism, separation, hate, vanity, seeming successes, and need to acquire, I have come to experience that I have always been (and infinitely will be) accepted by God. This knowing has also allowed me to accept others for who they are - imperfections and all. I see now that it was only when I could accept all of me - the same way God has always accepted me - that it was impossible not to accept others just as they are.

As I deepen my practice, Something Greater also helps me to better accept and honor my feelings - all of them - just as they are, and then let them go with grace. In turn, I find I am also able to accept others' emotions - just as they are. This has created a more connected and harmonious space for meaningful conversations in all of my relationships, and in particular, my relationship with my daughter, Emily.

Emily's Perspective on Acceptance

During this conversation with my dad, when I felt angry and afraid, I experienced a powerful shift. Because he didn't try to fix my situation or my stress, join me in my pity party, or hop on the blame train with me (#rude), I was able to lean into my feelings and face the situation from a place of personal responsibility. I was able to just be with myself, the experience, and my own feelings.

In years past if my dad refused to blame the other with me, I often interpreted his refusal as a judgment of me. I likely would have responded to the lack of "joining in" with some kind of inner dialogue like, "Okay, I get it. You're better than me because you're not judging." I'd tell myself that if he didn't want to join in, I'd go find someone else who could "stoop to my level" so that I could feel reassured that I was right and they were wrong!

Time and again I find that when I am blaming others for my experience, however, I am in avoidance mode; I'm avoiding my feelings. And when I avoid my feelings, I also avoid the reality of the moment. Which, in this case, was simply that this thing happened at work, and I didn't like it. While my mind argued that "the other" didn't understand how their decisions impacted me (along with a whole bunch of other stories), at the end of the day, the only truth I knew for sure was that I felt mad and scared. It became apparent that the longer I resisted these feelings, the more I suffered.

Tony deMello says that "suffering occurs when [we] clash with reality. When [our] illusions clash with reality, when [our] falsehoods clash with truth, then [we] have suffering. Otherwise there is no suffering."[22] I believe that when we avoid our feelings by blaming others, we deny a very powerful part of the human experience: the transformative nature of learning how to accept and love all of our feelings.

After lots of opportunities to practice letting go of blame, I notice now that when shit happens and life gets messy, I am more inclined to seek support from others (like my dad) who are willing to hold the space for my messiness without trying to fix it or hop on the blame train with me. As a result, I notice that I am better able to walk through life with grace and acceptance for what is.

This can be a scary concept, though. I can hear you wondering: what the heck are you talking about, Emily? You're telling me that you've experienced all of this sadness, grief, and heartache; that the WORLD is experiencing sadness, grief, and heartache, yet somehow you can say that all is well?

In my experience, accepting what is does NOT mean that I have to like the "mess" or the "bad" things that happen. It simply means that I am not resisting or trying to avoid the feelings underneath the "mess." Instead of being in resistance, I can choose to accept the situation for what it is - knowing that I don't necessarily have to like it or even be okay with it - and then take responsibility for the only thing I have control over: my feelings and how I choose to respond to the "mess."

I believe that inner work allows us to embark on an "unlearning" journey that ultimately leads to acceptance for all parts of ourselves - from the very best to the very worst - and for all of our feelings - from the most joyful to the most uncomfortable - in every moment and in every situation. I believe that the more we can simply accept what is - with ourselves, our situation, and in all of life - the more we can see that as Tony says, "all is well, all is well."[23]

Presence

"The key is to be here, fully connected with the moment, paying attention to the ordinary details of life."

- Pema Chödrön

In the Moment
Amidst the Pots and Pans

In April of 2021, Emily and Mike were preparing to share their thoughts on the presence chapter with each other at their weekly virtual meeting.

Because Mike was in physical pain, he took the call from the main living room area, adjacent to the kitchen, where he could sit in his recliner. His eldest daughter Sarah was nearby in the kitchen, very loudly cooking dinner.

"Pipe down back there!" Emily jokingly said to her sister from the other end of the call.

Mike, excited by a Richard Rohr quote he had found on Presence, opted to share the quote, rather than join in on the banter between his daughters.

"Em, listen to this quote," he said. "'When you're present, you will experience The Presence. But the problem is, we're almost always somewhere else: reliving the past or worrying about the future.'"

As Mike continued sharing his reflections on the quote, pots and pans clanked in the kitchen. Emily noticed both the noise in the background and her dad speaking calmly, and her mind wandered to an earlier time when noise during a call would've been much different for her dad. When she was a kid, something as simple as someone coughing while her dad was on the phone ordering a pizza would've resulted in a brash covering of the receiver and a very controlled, but on-the-verge-of-a-blow-up command to *go into the other room if you need to cough!*

Emily felt in awe of the juxtaposition of her dad's presence from the time when she was a twelve-year-old kid until now. It was as if she was witnessing some sort of side-by-side or before-and-after picture of her dad. On the one side was the dad she remembered from her childhood who would've reacted very differently to background noise during a call. On the other side was the dad who now sat peacefully in his recliner, present to his daughter and their project, and seemingly unfazed by anything.

"So how does that quote resonate with you, Em?" Mike asked Emily, who, in that moment, noticed herself present both to the memory of her dad and her own feelings and experience of his equanimity.

"Dad, I'm watching you, and I am so amazed at how completely unfazed you are by Sarah's shenanigans while we're trying to write," Emily shared.

Mike, who had noticed the noise all along, simply smiled and said: "I'm just grateful for what is. Whatever's happening will happen."

DAD'S PERSPECTIVE ON PRESENCE

If I could go back and talk to my younger self at those hectic times when I was trying to get kids to games on time, starting a business, and trying to hear while ordering a pizza, I'd let him know that if he can learn how to be present amidst all the noise of life, he might not have to wait until he's 57 and his kids are grown to finally begin to understand and embody presence.

In 2015, while on a break at The Living School in Albuquerque, I had my first experience of presence while sharing with one of my teachers, Jim Finley, about my wife's trauma and how it had impacted me. Jim responded by sharing the trauma he had experienced while he was a monk at Gethsemani. When Jim spoke, I felt deeply moved by his warm smile and the hope and presence he exuded. Jim ended our conversation with these five words: "The pedagogy of the relationship."

While at the time I had no intellectual understanding of the pedagogy (defined by Merriam-Webster as "the art, science, or profession of teaching"), I see now that the being-ness in my interaction with Jim was the pedagogy in action. It was as if God was talking to me through Jim's humility and vulnerability. In a way, the felt experience of Jim being with me helped me to cultivate my own presence from within - I just didn't fully understand what was happening at the time.

It wasn't until Emily reflected on *her* experience of *my* presence during our call, that I finally had the words for Jim's impact on me many years ago. I realized that it is in these moments of *being* in relationship - like with Jim and with my daughter - that God teaches us how to be present. Of course I heard the pots and pans clanging and Emily's comment to her sister. Of course there was a part of me that could have opted for a very different response. The difference today is that I now know that I always have the choice to *be* with others and present to life - regardless of the background noise.

Today I see that while it didn't seem like God was doing anything in the midst of all my distracting thoughts and feelings I experienced during my Centering Prayer practice, He was simply inviting me - without force or coercion - into His Presence. As He does nothing in these moments other than just be with me, it seems that paradoxically I receive so much in knowing that the Great Presence is always in me, working through me, and existing all around me.

For me, the pedagogy is what is unfolding in all of my relationships - with myself, with God, and with everyone and everything. I believe that all of our relationships - no matter how important or insignificant they may seem - teach us how to be Present; they teach us how to not know, to do nothing, and to let whatever is, just be. For me, "the pedagogy of relationship" is Presence.

As I reflect back on my younger self and the hustle and bustle of being a dad with four kids, I'd leave him with this advice:

Before your children wake each morning, take some time to sit in silence and be with God - even if it's for five minutes. Then set aside some time in the middle of the day - two minutes will do - to reflect and inquire about how you are *being* with your co-workers, your partner, your customers, and yourself. Ask yourself: are you *being* present to the Presence amidst all of life?

I'd tell him that it's okay to slow down, take a breath, and let go of the day before stepping into your home for the evening. I'd encourage him to consider that every time he returns home to his family, it's a chance to let go with God into a whole new moment and a whole new beginning. It's an opportunity to be present to all the ordinary details of life - pots clanging or not.

At the end of the day, I'd tell that 24-year-old version of myself that *things may not turn out exactly as you think they should, young man, but if you stay open to letting go of the formula and being present to not knowing, shifts will happen in your relationships that you never could have imagined would be possible.* I'd assure him that he will fail at all of this over and again, but that it's okay, because Presence isn't something he really has to strive for. Presence is and always has been available, in every moment, and each time he chooses to return to it, he will be reminded of the Love of all that is and that it's ok to just be.

Emily's Perspective on Presence

When I watched my dad during our call, I was struck by how 22 years later, my brain still expected the same response from him - the one that quietly demanded that we pipe down in the background because he was on a call.

At the same time I was expecting this response, I also noticed that my dad wasn't actually trying to control the noise around him. It's as if I was witnessing in real time just how much "this shit works" as I observed my dad's personal transformation in action.

I believe that my dad's warmth, calmness, and *being*ness, coupled with my own ability to be in the moment with myself *and* with him, is presence: the experience of *being* with another while also being with ourselves.

When we are present, our energy not only transforms our own experience of what is, but it also carries a contagious quality that invites others into the moment as well.

As we've explored throughout the book, so many of our habits and patterns - both conscious and unconscious - develop early on in life. These habits - like years of a parent giving "the look" to his child while ordering a pizza - don't just go away, they get embedded into our cellular memory. This is why 22 years later, as a grown woman, I still expected the same look I had received from my dad for so many years. Without awareness and the ability to observe our experience in real time, our conditioned responses can unknowingly take us out of the moment and disrupt our ability to be present.

I believe that it only takes one person to change the dynamic of years-long patterns of not being present to ourselves and one another. When one person chooses to shift out of unconscious patterns, not only does this create a palpable shift in that person, but it also invites others into the moment so they can experience shifts of their own. Recognizing that our ability to respond rather than react is a choice is directly correlated to our ability to experience presence both with ourselves and with another.

As we become more aware of our experience of presence (or lack thereof), we begin to also notice what is happening in our minds during the moments when we are taken out of presence. Once we recognize these habitual thought patterns - versus mindlessly reacting to them - we can then choose a new way of being.

When my dad responded differently to the pots and pans, something happened for me - it was almost like that experience disrupted the old, familiar neural pathways in my brain. As a result, my perception of the situation - and of myself - shifted. In a way, as I noticed my expectation dissolve for how I anticipated my dad to respond (based on past experiences), it was like I was rewiring my brain. As a result of opening to this new experience and the moment, I saw my ability to choose to not only be present to my dad, but also to what was happening in my own mind. In this way, I have experienced presence as a domino-like effect, in which one person's choice to be in the moment - like my dad in the recliner - inspires others to also be present - like me, on the receiving end of the call, observing my dad.

My most notable experience of this domino effect is every fall when I am graced with the opportunity to model conscious responding to my first-grade students. Inevitably, every year, seconds after the first spill of the year occurs, it's as if time stops. The room goes silent as all 24 kids whip their heads around, looking at me to react to the "big mess," anticipating a raised voice, a finger point, a scolding, or whatever response they have been conditioned to expect when something like this happens. This moment is one of my favorites because it's an opportunity to dissolve the kids' expectations of what happens when we make a mistake. Instead, I get to model presence.

"Ope, looks like it's time to learn how we clean up messes. I'll show you where to find the rags," I often say with a smile, followed by singing our mantra that's sung in a jolly tone, "Mistakes are how we learn!"

While I am directly teaching how to reframe a "mistake," I am also indirectly using calm energy to teach/show/invite them into my presence. In turn, not only do the students then embody the response themselves but THEY then help OTHER students when they find themselves in similar situations. It always amazes me how fast kids learn, because for the rest of the year, whenever something falls to the floor or water gets knocked over, inevitably I will hear a student say calmly to his or her fellow students, "That's okay. Here, let's clean this up."

When we model and embody the energy of presence (in this case, through play in the classroom), everyone around us is impacted in a positive way, because presence allows love to flow naturally. This is especially true for children.

As you begin to contemplate your own experience of presence, I invite you to get curious about how you respond to the noise in your own life - whether that be in the background of a conversation, over spilled water, or the self-talk in your own head. Do you habitually react and unconsciously expect things to be how they have always been, or do you open to the experience, embrace it, and allow it to teach you a new way of being?

At the end of the day, there will always be some kind of noise in life. While this noise can seemingly get in the way of the lives we want to live, it is paradoxically a necessity for living that life. I believe that the key to being present isn't eliminating the noise, instead it's being open to it, embracing it, being with it, and recognizing that when we are present to the ordinary details of the moment, we are not only fully immersed in Love, we become the invitation to Love.

Love

"Love is constantly creating future possibilities for the good of all concerned— even, and especially, when things go wrong. Love allows and accommodates everything in the human experience, both the good and the bad, and *nothing else can really do this.* Nothing."

- Richard Rohr

Returning to
What's Most Important

In 2011, as Emily prepared to move back to Cincinnati from Italy, her brother Matt prepared to move to San Francisco. One day on a Skype call with Mike and Emily, Matt noted that his move would end their year-long tradition of meeting on Thursday nights where they were able to see and hear each other in a new way.

"Wellllll, are you ready for the second string, dad?!" Emily asked with excitement. She had no idea she'd just proposed something that would begin a 10-year (and counting) weekly tradition. All she knew was that she was excited to spend time with her dad.

"Of course!" Mike said, also feeling eager to connect in a new way.

"Yeah, but you'll never actually replace the first string!" Matt joked with a smile

A few weeks later, Emily and Mike began their Father-Daughter-Thursday-Night Conversations at the same local chili parlor where Mike and Matt had met for the previous year: Price Hill Chili.

Emily felt frazzled as she pulled into the parking lot. She was running late, and she could hear her dad's voice in her mind: *Be sure to protect your car doors and park in a corner spot.* Emily rolled her eyes at the advice of her own mental chatter, yet found herself pulling into an end spot.

As Emily rushed into the restaurant and looked around for her dad, she heard her phone ring.

"I'm just finishing up an appointment," Mike said into the phone, in his businessman-like tone. "I'll be there in a few minutes. Find a high-top table and I'll see you soon."

Mike didn't think to acknowledge he was running late. He was the breadwinner for the family, after all. His mind was focused on his workday and the last conversation he'd had. He had clinched a deal that launched him into the top hundred in sales again this year.

Emily rolled her eyes as she looked around for a high-top table. Doesn't he know I've never been here before? She thought. I'm here by myself, I don't know what I'm doing, and now he's going to be late!

When Mike arrived ten minutes later, he set aside his thoughts about work, greeted Emily with a hug, and took a seat across from her at the table. He noticed a well of gratitude rise within him at the opportunity to be with his daughter.

Emily, feeling relieved and excited to see her dad, also set aside her thoughts. "So, what do we do now?!" she asked.

Mike wasn't sure what they would talk about or how the conversation would go, so he figured that just getting started was a good place to begin.

"We just talk, Em," he said with a smile.

DAD'S PERSPECTIVE ON LOVE

Ten years ago, although I was still unconsciously wrapped up in my "formula," I was very aware of a desire to reconnect in a new way with my daughter. I felt a willingness to lean into creating something new. I believe this leaning in was accepting the invitation from God/Love to lead me into unknowing; a choice that changed my relationships in ways that I never dreamed were possible.

What did leaning in look like for me? It was stepping into the unknown and letting go of what I thought I knew: what I understood about my role as a dad, what I thought was best for my daughter, and even what to say or how to start the conversation the very first day it began. This unknowing was a challenge, and I often fell back into my egoic "knowing" (and still do at times), because this is part of the spiritual journey. In time though, Love guided me out of a formula-driven connection with my daughter and into a more mutual way of being and relating.

For me, having a formula-driven connection with my daughter was merely a reflection of how I was still living in full-on achievement mode and looking to externalities for my happiness. Despite this unconscious way of being with myself and with my daughter, I see now that Love was still there, inviting me into experiencing Something New in my relationship with Emily.

My egoic need to prove that I was a top performer at work didn't seem to matter to God. Nor did it seem to matter that it hadn't even occurred to me to question whether being late would have any sort of impact on my daughter. In my experience this is because Love is there amidst all of this - the "good" and the "bad" - patiently waiting for us to lean into its invitation to create new possibilities.

Looking back, I can also see that my little bit of willingness to connect with my daughter in a new way was more powerful than any of my old unconscious programming, because once we open to it, Love always finds a way to transform our relationships - regardless of what it's up against or where we're at in life. As I allowed this acceptance from Love - of both the "good" *and* the "bad" in me - I was able to accept all of me. I believe this non-dual way of being *and* seeing creates a spaciousness for infinite possibilities in all relationships.

How this happens, how Love comes in and transforms us and our relationships, is quite a mystery, because Love is a mystery. So I can't tell you what will happen or how things will unfold in your life. What I can say is that if you want to be in relationship in a new way with yourself, your Higher Power, or someone else, choosing to lean into this desire and beginning right where you're at is all Love needs to begin creating infinite possibilities.

Ten years ago, God didn't take me and Emily to the Vatican or on some great quest to climb

Mount Everest to experience Love, nor did She wait until we'd rid ourselves of all our egoic patterns (spoiler alert: this isn't even possible). Instead, once we became willing to lean into Something New, Love met us right where we were at - right there at Price Hill Chili.

Emily's Perspective on Love

When my dad and I started having conversations, things weren't perfect. I still had resentment. I was still rolling my eyes at the thought of him telling me what to do, not realizing I was an adult with my own choices - including what advice to take from him or not.

The thing is, though, I see now that Love was always there even amidst the eye-rolling and the resentment. This is because Love is everything. Love is all of me. So it's okay if we're irritated, judgmental, or holding resentments, because having these negative feelings doesn't mean Love goes away or shuns us. Conversely, Love remains with us as an ever-constant stream, calling us to embrace *all* of ourselves and *all* of the others. All we have to do is choose to jump in and embrace it - even if we don't know what we're jumping into - because Love is always patiently waiting for us to let it in to do its thing.

Trusting that Love is doing its thing can be difficult because it doesn't mean that everything becomes perfect or that we don't have negative experiences. In fact, the more we open to Love, the more we begin to notice and consciously experience our emotional charges. Instead of turning away from these feelings, however, when we allow Love in, we now see we can choose to respond differently. I believe that Love is a moment-by-moment choice we can return to over and over again - even when we experience negative emotions, get stuck in our minds' stories, or experience resentment toward others.

In time, the more we continue to choose Love, the more possibilities we begin to experience in our lives; possibilities for connection, for healing, and for miracles. We find that as we allow Love in, the more our capacity to receive Love expands and the more shifts we experience both internally and externally. Eventually, because living a life centered in Love feels so much better than one filled with unconscious reactivity and programming, we find that ultimately it becomes easier to just choose Love.

For me, I see now that simply following the desire to connect with my dad all those years ago was choosing Love. I didn't know it then, but I see now that following the nudge to connect was accepting Love's invitation to work its magic. In my case, our weekly conversations were a container that helped me transform my relationship not only with my dad, but also with myself and with others.

At the end of the day, though, we don't have to have it all figured out or know exactly what's unfolding. All we have to do is choose to follow the nudges - to make that phone call, to have the uncomfortable conversation, to offer to be the second string in weekly conversations with your parent, or to do whatever thing you're being called to do - because Love is always right there, waiting with its invitation to join you in creating all kinds of experiences that you didn't even know were possible.

Afterword

Going into this project, we all agreed on one basic thing: no person or thing can cause us to feel a certain way - my feelings are in me, your feelings are in you. This understanding laid the groundwork for taking personal responsibility for our emotional experiences throughout the writing process - something that I believe was integral to a blame-free way of moving through old patterns and creating new relationships.

This process of having honest, authentic conversations with my dad and sister wasn't always easy. In fact, sometimes it was downright messy and uncomfortable (and it still can be!). And, it was also one of the most rewarding experiences I've ever had in relationship.

Not only did I get the chance to move through years-old patterns of reactivity with my dad and my sister, but I also got to feel deeply seen and heard. And, I got to see and hear them in a new way. It turns out that listening to your family members share about their childhood experiences can be a really powerful reminder that no matter how reactive (read: pissed off) I might feel in the heat of a family-of-origin moment, my parents and siblings are people with feelings, too. I see now that even during the most emotionally intense family interactions, everyone is (and always has been) doing the very best they can at any given moment.

When I accepted the invitation to help write this book, I had no idea that what I was really being invited into was an entirely new way of relating with my family. I had no idea that stepping into the minefield of emotion I once felt so scared to enter, was ultimately what led to co-creating relationships with my family that are now rooted in equality and compassion and the kind of Love that accepts and welcomes *all* of myself and *all* of the other - just as we are.

Sarah Schweppe, MSSA, LISW, CHWC

End Notes

1 Mello, Anthony de. *Awareness: The Perils and Opportunities of Reality*, Double Day, "Listen And Unlearn," page 16, 1990.

2 Mello, Anthony de. *Awareness: The Perils and Opportunities of Reality*, Double Day, "On Waking Up," page 5, 1990.

3 For more information on childhood trauma: https://www.samhsa.gov/child-trauma/understanding-child-trauma

4 Mello, Anthony de. *Awareness: The Perils and Opportunities of Reality*, Double Day, Intro "On Waking Up", 1990.

5 Mello, Anthony de. *Awareness: The Perils and Opportunities of Reality*, Double Day, "Four Steps to Wisdom", page 79, 1990.

6 Mello, Anthony de. *Awareness: The Perils and Opportunities of Reality*, Double Day, "Four Steps to Wisdom",page 81, 1990.

7 Mello, Anthony de. *Awareness: The Perils and Opportunities of Reality*, Double Day, "Sleepwalking",page 88, 1990.

8 Mello, Anthony de. *Awareness: The Perils and Opportunities of Reality*, Double Day, "How Happiness Happens," page 25, 1990.

9 For more information: www.goconscious.com/enneagram/

10 Jung, CG, *The Philosophical Tree* (1945) Collected Works 13: Alchemical Studies
Paragraph 335

11 Esposito, *Ron, and Ooten, Deborah. Lifting the Veil: Enneagram Meditations* by Deborah Ooten and Ron Esposito. https://www.goconscious.com/store/

12 For more information: http://www.centeringprayer.com/lectio_divina.htm

13 For more information: https://www.contemplative.org/contemplative-practice/centering-prayer/ Bourgeault, Cynthia. *Centering Prayer and Inner Awakening.* Cowley Publications, 2004.

14 Bourgeault, Cynthia. *"Centering Prayer and Attention of the Heart."* Atlas Serials, March 2009, pp 15-27, https://summerstudy.yale.edu/sites/default/files/bourgeault_attention_of_the_heart.pdf

15 Finley, Jim. *The Living School, Center for Action and Contemplation*, 2017. For more information on the living school: https://cac.org/living-school/living-school-welcome/.

16 Warmerdam, Gary Van, host. *"Happiness as Choice."* *The Awareness and Consciousness Podcast,* season number, episode 4, Gary van Warmerdam, 6 September 2006. https://pathwaytohappiness.com/blog/podcast/happiness-as-choice

17 Hay, Louise. *Mirror Work.* Hay House, 1984.

18 Holden, Robert. *Loveability: Knowing How to Love and Be Loved.* Hay House, 2014.

19 Bernstein, Gabrielle. *The Universe Has Your Back: Transform Fear to Faith.* Hay House, 2018

20 For more information: https://www.abraham-hicks.com or google "Abraham Hicks" and select a Youtube recording that speaks to you :)

21 Rohr, Richard. *"Paradox: The Stable Witness."* Richard Rohr's Daily Meditations, Center for Action and Contemplation, 30 July 2014, https://cac.org/category/daily-meditations/

22 Mello, Anthony de. *Awareness: The Perils and Opportunities of Reality,* Double Day, "Labels", page 36, 1990.

23 Mello, Anthony de. *Awareness: The Perils and Opportunities of Reality,* Double Day, Intro "On Waking Up", 1990.

Resources

Bernstein, G. (2016). *The Universe Has Your Back: How to Feel Safe and Trust Your Life No Matter What.* Hay House Inc.

Bourgeault, C. (2013). *The Holy Trinity and the Law of Three: Discovering the Radical Truth at the Heart of Christianity* (Illustrated ed.). Shambhala.

Bourgeault, C. (2020). *Eye of the Heart: A Spiritual Journey into the Imaginal Realm.* Shambhala.

Bourgeault, C. (2004). *Centering Prayer and Inner Awakening* (1st ed.). Cowley Publications.

DeMello, A. (2021). Awareness: *The Perils and Opportunities of Reality* by Anthony De Mello (1990) Paperback. Image Books.

Finley, J., & Merton, T. (2004). *Thomas Merton's Path to the Palace of Nowhere: The Essential Guide to the Contemplative Teachings of Thomas Merton. Sounds True.*

Keating, T. (2012). *Invitation to Love 20th Anniversary Edition: The Way of Christian Contemplation* (Anniversary ed.). Continuum.

Myss, C., Finley, J., PhD, & True, S. (2010). *Transforming Trauma: Uncovering the Spiritual Dimension of Healing.* Sounds True.

Ph.D., H. R. (2014). *Loveability.* Hay House Inc.

Rohr, R. (2003). *Everything Belongs: The Gift of Contemplative Prayer* (Revised and updated edition). Crossroad.

Rohr, R. (2011). *Breathing Under Water: Spirituality and the Twelve Steps.* Franciscan Media.

Rohr, R., Finley, J. Ph.D. (2013). *Intimacy The Divine Ambush. Center for Action and Contemplation.*

Schweppe, M. (2016). *Taking a Stand: 25 Insights to an Incredible Life.* Balboa Press.

About Us

Mike has been married to his partner, Sue, for 42 years. They have four adult children: Sarah, Christy, Emily, and Matt, and one cat named Batman. He served as the Activities/Athletic Director at Hillcrest School Residential Treatment Center for Juveniles before founding a small insurance and financial services business. He earned his Bachelor's degree from the College of Community Services at the University of Cincinnati and his M.Ed from XU in Counseling. From 2015-2017, Mike attended The Living School for Action and Contemplation (Albuquerque, NM) where he learned about integrating the Wisdom of the Perennial Traditions.

Mike loves being in community, spending time with his family, contemplative practices, working with his team and associates, serving customers, reading the mystics, and having conversations with other dads and daughters.

Emily is an elementary school teacher in her ninth year of teaching. She graduated from the University of Cincinnati with a North American Women's Studies degree in 2010 and completed her Master's Degree in Elementary Education from Xavier University in 2018. She incorporates Conscious Discipline and Trauma-Informed practices in her classroom.

Emily loves spending time with her family and friends, teaching, hiking with her husband, Drew and their dog Chance, reading, traveling, meditating, and deepening her spirituality practices.

www.ingramcontent.com/pod-product-compliance
Lightning Source LLC
Chambersburg PA
CBHW071432130726
47997CB00006B/2054